CHINCOTEAGUE
NATIONAL WILDLIFE REF
An Ecological Treasure

Photography and Text by Irene Hinke-Sacilotto

WESTCLIFFE PUBLISHERS
westcliffepublishers.com

CONTENTS

LOCATION

Access

Chincoteague National Wildlife Refuge (NWR) lies across the Assateague Channel from the town of Chincoteague, Virginia. To reach the refuge, take US 13 north from Norfolk, Virginia, or south from Salisbury, Maryland. Turn east on VA 175 and continue until you reach the town of Chincoteague. Follow Maddox Boulevard east to the refuge entrance.

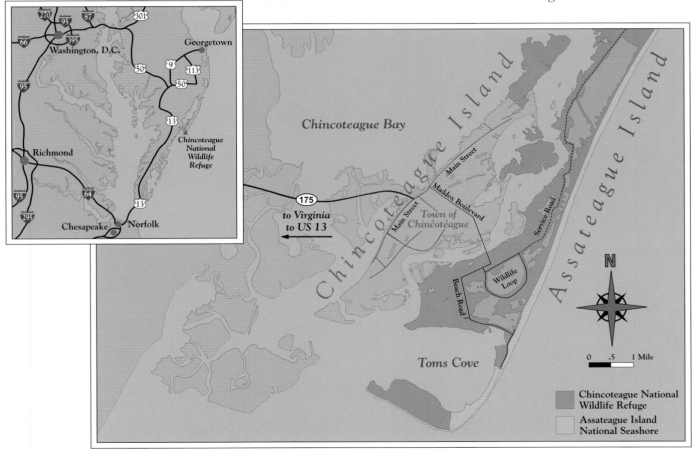

Chincoteague National Wildlife Refuge

Managed by the U.S. Fish and Wildlife Service, Chincoteague National Wildlife Refuge includes more than 14,000 acres of beach, dune, marsh, and maritime forest habitats. The majority of the refuge is located in Virginia on the southern end of the 37-mile-long barrier island of Assateague. Other refuge holdings include tracts on Wallops and Chincoteague Islands, several islands in Assateague Bay, and all or portions of barrier islands farther south—Assawoman, Metompkin, and Cedar.

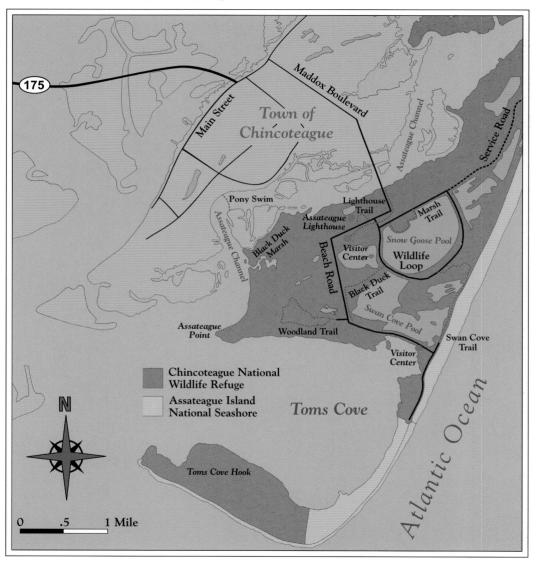

INTRODUCTION

Overview

Chincoteague National Wildlife Refuge was purchased in 1943 using revenues from the sale of Federal Duck Stamps. It is one of more than 540 refuges within the National Wildlife Refuge System. Larger than the National Park System, it includes more than 95 million acres, with at least one refuge in each state.

Origin

Chincoteague NWR was established to provide habitat for migratory birds, particularly the then-dwindling population of greater snow geese. Today, the refuge is managed for the benefit of a variety of wildlife and plant species, some of them endangered or threatened. Strategically located along the Atlantic Flyway, the refuge serves as a vital resting and feeding area for millions of migratory birds, including the large numbers of snow geese that stop at the refuge during fall migration.

Visitation

Within a day's drive from eight major metropolitan areas on the East Coast, Chincoteague NWR sees approximately 1.5 million visitors each year, with people traveling from as many as 50 states and 43 countries. Within the National Wildlife Refuge System, Chincoteague is one of the most popular destinations. Its hiking and biking trails, wildlife drive, visitor center, and interpretive programs offer visitors outstanding opportunities to observe and learn about wildlife and barrier island ecology.

Importance

- Major staging area for migratory shorebirds
- Key migratory stop for waterfowl, warblers, songbirds, and peregrine falcons
- Critical nesting area for the dwindling populations of piping plovers and least terns
- Habitat for the endangered Delmarva Peninsula fox squirrel

Bird Species

Blue-winged teal are small dabbling ducks that nest on the refuge, along with gadwalls, black ducks, Canada geese, mallards, and other species. They are one of the more than 300 species of birds observed on the refuge.

Management Programs

- Protect and restore threatened and endangered species
- Ensure adequate resting and feeding sites for shorebirds, waterfowl, and other migratory birds
- Preserve the natural diversity and abundance of native flora and fauna
- Provide opportunities for environmental education and wildlife-related recreation

Wetlands Protection

Since the early 1900s, development, drainage, and pollution have destroyed more than 50 percent of U.S. coastal wetlands, significantly reducing the amount of suitable resting, feeding, and nesting areas for waterfowl, shorebirds, and other wildlife. Chincoteague and other national wildlife refuges play a crucial role in preserving our nation's remaining wetlands. For example, with more than 500,000 shorebirds visiting each spring, Chincoteague NWR is one of the top five shorebird migration staging areas east of the Rockies.

Brief History

The first to visit Assateague Island were Native Americans who seasonally hunted, fished, and gathered plants here. In the 1600s, settlers from the mainland grazed livestock on the island to avoid taxes and fencing regulations. In the 1800s, Assateague Village was established near the site of the present-day Assateague Lighthouse. Prospering from oystering and commercial fishing, the town grew. At the turn of the last century, the population had reached 225. Its decline began in the 1920s when the island's new owner blocked shell road access to Toms Cove. Over time, the villagers left the island, many floating their homes on barges across the channel to Chincoteague Island.

The Fields family, principal owners of Assateague Island, sold the property in 1943 to the U.S. government to be set aside as a national wildlife refuge.

ASSATEAGUE LIGHTHOUSE

The first lighthouse on the island was constructed in 1833 to warn ships of dangerous offshore shoals, which were responsible for multiple shipwrecks. In 1867, the original 42-foot-high lighthouse was replaced by the taller 142-foot structure seen today. Operated by the U.S. Coast Guard, the lighthouse is opened seasonally to the public.

Assateague Island National Seashore

In 1965, Congress established Assateague Island National Seashore to protect one of North America's few remaining undisturbed beaches along the Atlantic Coast. This pristine shoreline provides piping plovers and other shorebirds with vital feeding and nesting habitat. The national seashore covers all of Assateague Island and adjacent bays.

The Virginia end of the island is owned and managed by the Chincoteague National Wildlife Refuge. However, in the Toms Cove area, the National Park Service assists the refuge in managing public use.

BARRIER ISLAND DYNAMICS

Role of Barrier Islands

Barrier islands are narrow ribbons of sand lying between the ocean and the mainland. Their beaches and shallow bays serve as buffers, protecting inland areas from damage. By their very nature, barrier islands are dynamic. They move and change appearance in response to ocean currents, storms, and rising sea levels.

Island Migration

Like all barrier islands, Assateague Island is slowly moving. Longshore currents sweep sand from the north end of the island south. In the last hundred years, Assateague Island has migrated more than 2.5 miles south, forming Toms Cove Hook. For perspective, consider that the present-day lighthouse and old Coast Guard station were once situated at the southern tip of the island. Today, tons of sand separate both from the end of the hook, and trees surround the inland lighthouse.

Land Formation

Sometimes during violent storms, the sea breaches the dunes and floods low areas, transporting tons of sand to back bays and marshes. Over time, grasses and other pioneer plants take root in the new deposits, their roots and runners trapping more sediment and attracting other plants and organisms. By this process, land is added to the western shore of Assateague and the island slowly migrates toward the mainland. Toms Cove, once navigable by ships, has filled with sediment and is too shallow for passage.

Ancient Marsh

East of Assateague lie the remnants of an ancient marsh once part of the island. A victim of the island's westward migration, this marsh now rests beneath the sea. Sometimes during storms, pieces of the peat-like material wash ashore, providing willets and other birds with a place to perch above the surf.

Seasonal Change

The beaches change appearance with the seasons. In the summer, they widen as longshore currents and gentle waves deposit sand. In the winter, they narrow and become steeper as storms wash tons of sand out to sea.

The most dramatic changes on barrier islands are the result of violent storms and hurricanes. Strong winter storms known as nor'easters erode the shoreline, leaving beaches narrow and steep. Some of the dunes you see today on Assateague are man-made, constructed after a 1962 nor'easter removed much of the island's natural foredune.

The Inevitable

By their nature, barrier islands are unstable. Attempts to stop their natural migration with jetties, snow fences, or artificial dunes are futile. Past efforts to stabilize Assateague Beach have proven ineffective. Severe storms have caused roads, trails, parking lots, and buildings to be moved farther inland.

HABITATS

- Beach and Dunes
- Shrub Community
- Maritime Forest
- Coastal Marshes
- Assateague and Chincoteague Bays
- Impoundments

Beach and Dunes

INTERTIDAL ZONE

At the water's edge, the intertidal zone is alternately covered by seawater and exposed as the waves advance and recede. The inhabitants are hardy, able to withstand breaking waves and shifting sand. Abundant in the surf, phyto- and zooplankton provide food for shrimp, clams, crabs, and other organisms.

Mole Crab

Well suited to the intertidal zone, mole crabs ride ashore on advancing waves, burrow backward in the sand, and expose featherlike antennae to filter plankton from receding waves.

Sea Treasures

Retreating waves leave behind shells, seaweed, coral, egg casings, arrowheads, sharks' teeth, and other treasures. Storms often litter the beach with hundreds of shells, of which the knobbed whelk is the largest and one of the most beautiful.

Sanderling

At the water's edge, sanderlings are a familiar sight, chasing retreating waves as they feed on mole crabs and other organisms in the wet sand. Although small, they are feisty when defending their stretch of beach.

SUPRATIDAL ZONE

The supratidal zone extends from the intertidal zone to the dunes. The beach is a crucial feeding area for thousands of migrating shorebirds. High tides deposit plant and animal debris at the extreme upper tide line. This beach wrack provides food and shelter for tiny shrimp, worms, insects, and large numbers of small crustaceans known as beach fleas.

Ruddy Turnstone

Named for their feeding habits, ruddy turnstones use their bills to flip over shells, small stones, and grains of sand in search of food.

Willet

Willets breed on the refuge and are common visitors to the marshes and beaches. Their shrill calls are easy to recognize.

Ghost Crab

On summer evenings when the temperature drops, ghost crabs emerge from their burrows. They race to the sea to wet their gills and by moonlight feed on decaying animals, mole crabs, beach fleas, and other organisms washed ashore or buried in the sand.

DUNES

The process of dune formation begins when the wind transports fine particles of sand from the beach and overwash fans to areas beyond the high tide line. Where airborne particles encounter a plant, shell, piece of driftwood, or other obstacle, they are deposited. Sand continues to accumulate and forms ridges. Over time, American beach grass becomes established on the rudimentary dune. Its roots and underground runners trap sand and further stabilize the surface. An important first line of defense against storm surges, dunes protect inland areas from flooding and salt-sensitive habitat from invasion by seawater.

Plant Adaptations

The dunes are inhospitable places to live, with soaring summer temperatures and constant battering by the wind and salt spray. Water percolates through the sand quickly, leaving the surface dry and poor in nutrients. Constantly shifting sand buries new growth.

Some plants have evolved to survive in this harsh environment. Special adaptations include:

- Leaf blades that absorb nutrients from the salt spray
- Long taproots to access freshwater deep within the ground
- Compact, ground-hugging shapes that protect against the wind
- Thick leaves with a waxy coating to conserve water
- Surfaces covered with a fine coating of hairs to combat the hot sun
- Flexible blades that bend in the wind, tracing circular patterns in the sand

Avoid walking on dunes. Your footsteps can damage the plants and underground runners that help stabilize the sand.

Piping Plover

The piping plover is federally classified as a threatened species. Because of human disturbance and loss of nesting habitat, its population has dropped to a dangerously low level. To assist the piping plover recovery on the refuge, access to nesting habitat is restricted. Biologists place protective closures around nests, monitor chicks, and control predators such as grackles, ravens, and foxes.

Piping and Wilson's plovers, common and least terns, black skimmers, willets, and oyster-catchers nest on uninhabited beaches and are easily disturbed by intruders. Hikers or ORV users can unwittingly crush the birds' speckled eggs, which blend with their surroundings. **Please obey all "Closed to the Public" signs posted to protect these birds.**

Shrub Community

In shrub communities, found inland from the primary dunes, plants are sheltered from salt spray, wind, and flooding. Away from the sea, small trees, vines, and shrubs are able to survive and develop into dense thickets, the exact composition varying with elevation, proximity to the ocean, and availability of freshwater. Bayberry, wax myrtle, poison ivy, Virginia creeper, winged sumac, greenbrier, black-berry, and groundsel trees form a nearly impenetrable tangle of vines and branches. They provide shelter for white-tailed deer, foxes, opossums, Eastern cottontails, raccoons, and other small mammals.

SHRUB COMMUNITY INHABITANTS

Poison Ivy

Poison ivy is common in the thickets and wooded areas of Chincoteague National Wildlife Refuge. Its leaves and berries serve as a valuable food source for wildlife. Turning crimson in the fall, its three distinctive leaflets warn humans to stay away.

Brown Thrasher

Brown thrashers, catbirds, cardinals, yellow warblers, and Eastern towhees are among the birds that reside on the refuge year-round and depend on the thickets for food, shelter, and nest sites.

Northern Bobwhite

Bobwhites are often seen feeding in grassy areas adjacent to thickets, where they retreat into the thick brush if threatened. For protection, they often travel in family groups known as coveys.

Yellow-Rumped Warbler

During fall migration, yellow-rumped warblers, as well as other warblers and songbirds, rely on the thickets for insects, rose hips, berries, seeds, and other food to fuel their journey.

Eastern Kingbird

From perches overlooking fields and open water, Eastern kingbirds hunt insects. Their white-tipped tail feathers distinguish these agile fliers.

Blue Grosbeak

Blue grosbeaks breed on the refuge and take advantage of the abundant supply of seeds, berries, and insects to feed their young.

Eastern Cottontail

Along with various small mammals, Eastern cottontails rely on the thickets for cover and protection from such predators as foxes and hawks.

Red Fox

When hunting, red foxes use the thicket's dense underbrush for cover, enabling them to surprise rabbits, waterfowl, ground-nesting birds, and other small prey.

Maritime Forest

Away from the sea on old dunes that form the more stable part of the island, the milder conditions allow trees to grow. Dominated by loblolly pine, the upland forest community also includes mixed stands of hardwoods—red and water oak, red maple, American holly, black cherry, common persimmon, sassafras, and sweet gum. The forest's bounty of seeds, pinecones, acorns, buds, nuts, and berries is a valuable source of food for a variety of animals.

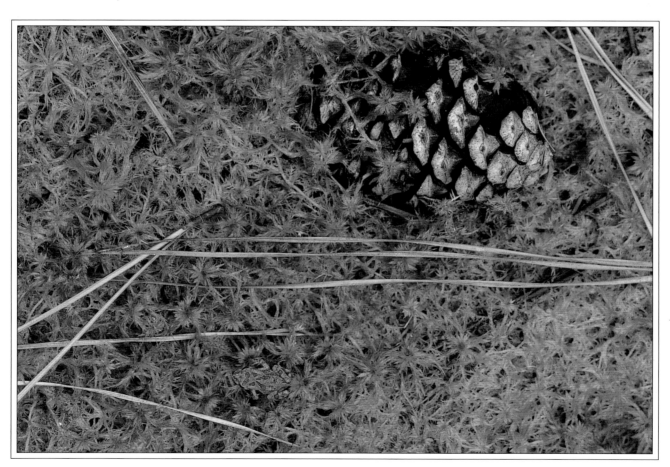

IMPORTANCE

During severe storms, the forest acts as a windbreak, shielding the mainland from damage and providing shelter for wildlife. In summer, the trees offer animals shade and relief from the heat.

On the refuge, dead and decaying trees are left undisturbed because they recycle nutrients to the soil and provide homes for Delmarva Peninsula fox squirrels, raccoons, opossums, screech owls, woodpeckers, chickadees, wood ducks, and other cavity-nesting birds.

MANAGEMENT

The refuge manages the forest to maintain biological diversity and provide habitat for Delmarva Peninsula fox squirrels, cavity-nesting birds, woodcocks, and migrating hawks, warblers, and other songbirds. As the forest understory matures, the vegetation becomes less nutritional and less palatable to wildlife. A thick mat of pine needles covers the floor and inhibits new growth. To rejuvenate the forest and encourage the growth of plants more valuable to wildlife, the refuge staff thins stands of trees and uses prescribed burning to remove undesirable litter and brush.

Southern Pine Beetle Infestation

The Southern pine beetle cyclically invades the pine forests of the South. Stands that are overstocked, past their prime, or damaged by drought, saltwater intrusion, and storms are particularly susceptible to infection. To prevent the spread of the infestation, affected trees are cut down and burned.

Reforestation

Compared to pure stands of loblolly pine, a mixed forest of pine and hardwoods is more valuable to wildlife and is less susceptible to disease. To revitalize the forest, biologists and volunteers plant seedlings of oak, persimmon, dogwood, and other beneficial hardwoods.

FRESHWATER PONDS

Throughout the forest and thickets are numerous small freshwater ponds. Shaded and sheltered from the wind and salt spray, these nutrient-rich pools support large populations of microscopic organisms, fish, mosquito larvae, dragonflies, beetles, and other aquatic insects. A common visitor is the bullfrog, the largest frog in North America.

Freshwater pools make a good place to look for animals such as frogs, snakes, herons, raccoons, and deer, all attracted by plentiful food and potable water.

MARITIME FOREST INHABITANTS

Pink Lady's Slipper

In the shade of the forest, crested yellow orchids and pink lady's slippers thrive in the acid soil created by decaying pine needles.

Fowler's Toad

Common along forest trails, Fowler's toads share the refuge with fellow amphibians including Southern leopard frogs, bullfrogs, green tree frogs, and redback salamanders. Fowler's toads feed on the sow bugs, spiders, beetles, and other insects found beneath the leaf litter on the forest floor. The rough texture and blotchy coloration of their skin provide them with camouflage and protection from predators.

Black Rat Snake

Snakes found on the refuge include the black racer, Eastern and Southern hognose, Eastern garter, brown and Northern water snake, and the black rat snake, identifiable by its white chin and black coloration. The black rat snake is an excellent climber and often resides in high tree cavities. With a diet of small prey including mice, frogs, insects, and eggs, snakes play an important role in nature's system of checks and balances. Although no poisonous snakes make their home on the refuge, any snake can inflict a nasty bite if provoked.

Great Crested Flycatcher

Expert fliers, great crested flycatchers snatch from the air moths, dragonflies, grasshoppers, bees, and other airborne insects that make up their diet.

Tree Swallows

Nesting boxes have been placed through-out the refuge to supplement natural tree cavities. The species benefiting include tree swallows, screech owls, wood ducks, and endangered Delmarva Peninsula fox squirrels.

A welcome sight on the refuge, swallows are nature's way of controlling the mosquito population.

Falcons and Hawks

During fall migration, raptors such as Cooper's and sharp-shinned hawks, peregrine falcons, kestrels, and merlins stop on the refuge to rest and feed before continuing to their final destination. From perches high in trees and dead snags, raptors like this Cooper's hawk use their keen eyesight to spot rodents and other prey in the fields and marshes below.

White-Tailed Deer

With much of the forest understory relatively open, white-tailed deer can move about freely and browse on tender new shoots, buds, and the leaves of such low-growing plants as greenbrier and poison ivy.

Sika Deer

Not native to North America, sika deer are Asian elk. In 1920, a few were released on the north end of Assateague. Adapting well to their new environment, they spread across the island. Today, they are hunted to keep their numbers in check. Without control, the sika deer threaten forest regeneration by eating seedlings and other new growth. Compared with the native white-tailed deer, sika deer are smaller, darker, and spotted. They have a "powder-puff" rump with a small tail. Like antelope, they spring, rather than run, when startled.

Wild Ponies

After several hundred years roaming free on Assateague Island, the "wild Chincoteague ponies" have evolved into a small, sturdy stock. Their heavy, shaggy coats insulate them from the wind and cold. With bellies bloated from a diet high in salt, they appear perpetually pregnant.

Some believe the ponies escaped from the wreck of a Spanish galleon, but more likely they are the descendants of colonists' horses left to graze on the island in the 1600s. The colonists used the island as a natural corral and a means of avoiding taxes.

Herd Management

The Chincoteague Volunteer Fire Company owns the ponies. The number grazing on the refuge is limited by permit. Fences restrict the ponies' movement, keeping them out of sensitive areas and from competing with wildlife for food. Unpredictable, these wild horses kick and bite, so keep your distance.

Pony Penning

Each July during "Pony Penning," the "saltwater cowboys" of the Chincoteague Volunteer Fire Company round up the horses. On horseback, they drive the herd across Assateague Channel to Chincoteague Island, where they sell the foals and yearlings at auction.

Cattle Egret

In contrast with other fish-eating wading birds, cattle egrets have shorter bills better suited to their diet of insects, frogs, toads, and mollusks. They frequently follow the ponies as they feed along the edge of the forest. Cattle egrets eat insects flushed from the grasses by the horses' hooves, or, by hitching a ride, they feed on the ticks and other parasites attached to a pony's hide.

Delmarva Peninsula Fox Squirrel

Compared with gray squirrels, fox squirrels are larger with bushier tails and spend more time on the ground. Once, Delmarva Peninsula fox squirrels ranged from central New Jersey south through eastern Pennsylvania and down the Delmarva Peninsula. When forests were cleared for homes and farms, the squirrel's numbers dropped drastically. Today, this species is classified as endangered. Between 1969 and 1971, 30 squirrels were moved to Chincoteague NWR in an attempt to restore their population. Since the squirrels' relocation, their number on the refuge has increased nearly tenfold.

Fox Squirrel Management

Delmarva Peninsula fox squirrels prefer living in a forest with an open under-story and a mix of loblolly pine and hardwoods, where food sources such as nuts, berries, seeds, and fungi are plentiful. To aid in the squirrels' recov-ery, the refuge manages the forest to favor their habitat needs and food requirements. Undisturbed areas are set aside for the squirrels, and pets are banned from the refuge. Nesting boxes provided for the squirrels supplement natural tree cavities.

On the refuge, please drive slowly and remain alert to avoid further reducing the Delmarva Peninsula fox squirrel population.

Coastal Marshes

CREATION

Where the sea encounters the calm waters of shallow bays, it loses forward momentum and drops its load of silt and sand, creating mudflats and sandbars. Over time, such marsh plants as cordgrass and sedges colonize the new surface. The landmass grows as roots and underground runners trap more sediment and mats of algae, mollusks, and other organisms stabilize the surface. Slowly, open water evolves into a marsh.

VALUE

Salt marshes provide habitat for migratory birds and other wildlife, as well as nourishment for a wide range of aquatic organisms. They slow the flow of water to prevent flooding and replenish the ground-water supply. The plants trap sediment, absorb impurities and excess nutrients, and thereby improve water quality.

NUTRIENT RECYCLING

When marsh grass dies, it decomposes and releases organic matter, or detritus, and nutrients into the water. These products of decay are flushed through the tidal guts into the channels and bays, where they support large populations of phyto- and zooplankton. These become food for shrimp, periwinkles, clams, crabs, oysters, and other aquatic organisms including the larval and embryonic stages of commercially valuable fish and shellfish.

LOW MARSH

In the lower sections of the marsh, life is difficult. Organisms must be able to tolerate intermittent flooding, large fluctuations in salinity, limited oxygen, and an unstable substrate. Occupants must adapt to survive. The predominant plant of the low marsh, saltmarsh cordgrass, tolerates the high salinity by excreting excess salt through its blades. Its extensive system of underground runners anchors the grass in place and stabilizes the banks of tidal guts. Wading birds like this yellow-crowned night heron dine in the marsh on small fish, fiddler crabs, and mollusks exposed at low tide.

HIGH MARSH

A fine grass known as saltmeadow cordgrass (saltmeadow hay) grows at higher elevations in the marsh where flooding is only periodic. Other plants found sharing this habitat include spike grass, sea-lavender, and black needlerush. The laughing gull conceals its nest in the salt-tolerant grasses of the high marsh, as do willets, herring gulls, ducks, and other species that frequent the marsh.

COASTAL MARSH INHABITANTS

Black-Necked Stilt

Black-necked stilts feed in the shallows and use their slender bills to pick up seeds, tiny fish, insects, mosquito larvae, and other small organisms.

Clapper Rail

As the tide recedes, clapper rails emerge from the cordgrass onto the mudflats to feed on crabs, snails, and other invertebrates. Their long toes distribute their weight and keep them from sinking into the soft mud. When faced with danger, they prefer to run for cover rather than fly.

Great Blue Heron

The largest of the North American herons, the great blue heron stands 4 feet tall. Although primarily a fish-eater, it will consume eels, frogs, crawfish, insects, snakes, and even small rodents.

Red-Bellied Turtle

Turtles are cold-blooded and externally regulate their body temperature. Red-bellied turtles, like their relatives, warm themselves in the sun so they can digest food, move easily, and perform other bodily functions.

Snapping Turtle

Formidable predators, snapping turtles ambush fish, frogs, snakes, ducklings, and small mammals from the cover of aquatic vegetation. The saw-toothed ridge along its tail and shell make this large turtle easy to identify.

In a flash, a snapping turtle can strike with powerful jaws capable of breaking bones and causing serious injury. Be sure to keep your distance.

Raccoon

Along tidal creeks and roadside ditches, raccoons forage for such delicacies as mussels, crabs, clams, cray-fish, fish, frogs, and turtle eggs. With sensitive fingers, they probe the bottom and locate food by touch.

Muskrat

With waterproof coats, partially webbed hind feet, and rudderlike tails, muskrats are excellent swimmers. Their domelike lodges appear throughout the marsh.

Saltwort

Saltwort (Salicornia) is an unusual-looking succulent plant. Able to store large amounts of water, it can survive in the saline soil found in the drier, sandy portions of the marsh. It is beautiful in the fall when its fleshy stems turn ruby red.

Wildflowers

Flowering plants produce seeds, berries, and fruits that are valuable food for wild-life. In the spring and summer, the blooms of blue-eyed grass, meadow beauty, narrow-leaved loosestrife, prickly pear cactus, saltmarsh fleabane, toadflax, rose mallow, and marsh pink add color to the refuge landscape.

Close examination of wildflowers such as this marsh pink reveals beautiful details that typically go unnoticed by the casual observer.

Assateague and Chincoteague Bays

Protected by Assateague Island, the relatively calm waters of Chincoteague and Assateague Bays are well suited as nurseries for fish and marine animals too small and vulnerable to survive in the ocean during the early stages of their development. Continuously replenished by the tide, food and nutrients abound. In sheltered areas where the water is warm and the bottom is rich in organic matter, widgeon grass, eelgrass, and other aquatic plants thrive. These plants create underwater forests that provide a safe haven for crabs, rays, snails, shrimp, worms, oysters, clams, and fish.

BAY INHABITANTS

Spider Crab

Spider crabs live on the bottom of shallow bays. Stiff hairs, spines, knobs, and a coating of bacteria and algae cover their shells. To this surface, sponges, seaweeds, tubeworms, and other organisms attach themselves and provide the crab with camouflage from predators and prey.

Brant

The large beds of eelgrass and widgeon grass make Assateague Channel and Toms Cove critical feeding areas for wintering and migrating brant.

American Oystercatcher

The American oystercatcher feeds at low tide on exposed oyster bars. Using its specialized bill, it opens oyster shells by severing the oyster's abductor muscle, and then removes the meat.

TOMS COVE

Horseshoe Crabs

Originating more than 350 million years ago, the horseshoe crab is a distant relative of spiders and scorpions. The crab is harmless; its spiked tail is not a weapon but serves as a rudder and tool to right the crab if it is flipped on its back. In May and June when the tide is high and the moon is full, female crabs swim into the inlets along the Mid-Atlantic Coast to spawn. Along the shoreline of Toms Cove, females lay their eggs in the soft sand near the high-water mark. Males follow and fertilize the eggs.

Migrating Shorebirds

Each spring, more than a million shorebirds fly from places as far south as Tierra del Fuego to their breeding grounds in the Arctic. By mid-May, the birds reach the shores of Toms Cove and the Delaware Bay. Exhausted and hungry, the birds arrive just in time to take advantage of the feast provided by the spawning horseshoe crabs.

Critical Habitat

For nearly two weeks, shorebirds such as ruddy turnstones (shown here), red knots, dunlins, and sanderlings gorge themselves on protein-rich horseshoe crab eggs. Nearly doubling their weight, they acquire the fat reserve necessary to complete their journey north. With such a high percentage of the shorebird population present at one time, the birds are extremely vulnerable to human disturbance, pollution, and natural disasters.

Red Knot

Birds are banded to help researchers learn about their distribution, migration patterns, life span, and habits. The colorful bands on the legs of this red knot are easily identified at a distance.

Diamondback Terrapin

Once served in local restaurants, diamondback terrapins are no longer commercially harvested and are protected on the refuge. Each spring, these salt-tolerant turtles emerge from the marshes to lay their eggs on the sandy beaches of Toms Cove.

Impoundments

DIKES AND BORROW DITCHES

As part of refuge management, wetlands were created through the construction of dikes around portions of the barrier flats. The 14 fresh/brackish water impoundments (also referred to as pools or moist soil management units) that resulted provide forage for waterfowl, feeding and resting areas for migrating shorebirds, and habitat for a variety of wildlife.

BORROW DITCHES

Ditches created as a result of dike construction form a system of waterways known as borrow ditches. In times of drought, they retain water when surrounding areas are dry, becoming havens for wading birds and waterfowl.

MANAGEMENT

Structures in the dikes allow the impoundment water levels to be adjusted to favor vegetation and conditions beneficial to wildlife. In the late winter and spring, impoundments are drained to create mudflat-type habitat for feeding and resting migratory shorebirds. The lower water level also concentrates food for wading birds and promotes the growth of plants valuable to waterfowl. At the end of the summer, rainwater is allowed to fill the impoundments and create conditions attractive to migrating and wintering ducks, geese, and swans.

END OF SUMMER

During severe summer droughts, the water in the borrow ditches becomes warm and depleted in oxygen. Oxygen-starved aquatic organisms seek relief at the surface and fall easy prey to a variety of animals such as black-crowned night herons.

WILDLIFE LOOP

The 3.25-mile Wildlife Loop around one of the larger impoundments provides visitors with excellent wildlife-viewing opportunities. The loop connects to hiking trails and is open to foot and bike traffic all day. At limited times, it is open to vehicles.

IMPOUNDMENT INHABITANTS

Greater Snow Goose

During fall migration, large flocks of swans, ducks, and geese stop at Chincoteague NWR to rest and feed. Typically in November, the number of snow geese on the refuge peaks, reaching more than 40,000 in some years. On the refuge, the snow geese feed on the rhizomes and roots of marsh grasses. When large numbers concentrate in a small area for a long time, the geese can damage a marsh, leaving behind bare mud and open water.

Black-Crowned Night Heron

Food concentrates near the water-control structures in the dikes, attracting a variety of animals including raccoons, ducks, grebes, loons, and wading birds such as this black-crowned night heron.

Green Heron

When fishing, herons move stealthily through the water to avoid alerting their prey. Green herons and other wading birds can extend their necks an amazing distance to strike at fish with lightning speed.

Mallard Drake

Like other birds, mallards meticulously care for their feathers, which are essential for their survival. They spend hours preening, and once finished, they rid themselves of loose feathers by ruffling them or flapping their wings.

Black Skimmers

As they fly up and down waterways, black skimmers extend their long lower mandible into the water to scoop up fish. They nest in colonies, laying their eggs in shallow scrapes on sand or oyster-shell beaches. Their chicks are light in color with blotchy markings that help them blend easily with their surroundings.

Brown Pelicans

Brown pelicans are familiar sights as they glide over the ocean with their wing tips just above the waves. They visit the impoundments and breed nearby in colonies along the Virginia coast.

Belted Kingfisher

The belted kingfisher hunts from branches overhanging waterways. When it spots a fish, it plunges head-first into the water in pursuit. The belted kingfisher's rattlelike call is quite distinctive, often announcing the bird's presence before it is seen.

Glossy Ibis

Bird bills vary in shape and size according to the bird's diet. The glossy ibis has a long, curved bill, the perfect tool to probe for organisms beneath the mud's surface.

Double-Crested Cormorant

Because the double-crested cormorant's feathers are not water-repellent, they require drying in the sun. These birds are excellent swimmers, able to stay underwater for long periods of time while in pursuit of fish, glass eels, and other marine life.

Ruddy Duck

Ruddy ducks frequent the borrow ditches, where they feed on aquatic vegetation, insect larvae, snails, and other invertebrates. These small diving ducks are readily identifiable by their long, stiff tails, which they use as a rudder while swimming underwater.

Tundra Swans

Tundra swans are native to Virginia. Their long necks enable them to feed on submerged aquatic vegetation. During the fall migration from their Arctic breeding grounds, they typically reach the refuge in November. After a brief stay, most move farther south for the winter.

Peregrine Falcon

Like other falcons, peregrines have long, pointed wings and slender tails. They can dive at remarkable speeds and catch small birds in midair. During fall migration, they stop at the refuge to rest and hunt over the North Wash Flats and adjacent beach.

Once nearly wiped out by DDT, the peregrine population has recovered with the help of a captive breeding/release program. In 1980, hand-raised peregrine chicks were brought to Chincoteague NWR and released from a hacking tower near the North Wash Flats. Annually, pairs have returned to this location to raise their young.

River Otter

River otters live in the refuge marshes and impoundments. With sleek bodies, webbed toes, and long, thick tails, they move through the water with ease as they track down meals of assorted organisms including fish, crabs, and mussels. Where they regularly enter and exit the water, they flatten vegetation into a noticeable slide.

SEASONAL HIGHLIGHTS

Winter

- Peaceful, with fewer visitors
- Wintering ducks, geese, grebes, loons, shorebirds, and black-backed gulls
- Resident songbirds (including warblers), woodpeckers, and other species
- Limited foliage, allowing easier wildlife viewing
- Waterfowl departure in March

Spring

- Spring wildflowers
- Arrival of migrating songbirds in April and May
- Spawning horseshoe crabs from May to early June
- Arrival of migrating gulls, terns, and shorebirds from May to early June
- Waterfowl breeding season and the appearance of the first ducklings and goslings

Summer

- Peak usage of the beach by vacationers
- Lighthouse tours (Check at the Herbert H. Bateman Educational and Administrative Center for details; see "Making the Most of Your Visit.")
- Pony roundup in late July
- Appearance of southward-migrating shorebirds from mid-July to mid-August
- Large concentrations of herons and other waders

Fall

- Arrival of neotropical migrants in September and October
- Raptor migration in September and October
- Fall waterfowl migration from October through December
- Monarch butterfly migration

MAKING THE MOST OF YOUR VISIT

- Take a hike or bike ride along the trails, beachcomb, or join an interpretive guide for a nature walk.

- Explore the Herbert H. Bateman Educational and Administrative Center. Enjoy the exhibits and consult with the knowledgeable staff to learn about refuge habitats and wildlife.

- Refer to field guides, books, and refuge brochures to better understand what you are observing.

Contact Information

Chincoteague Nat'l Wildlife Refuge
P.O. Box 62
Chincoteague Island, VA 23336
(757) 336-6122
http://chinco.fws.gov/

SPECIAL EVENTS

- International Migratory Bird Celebration: Mother's Day Weekend
- National Fishing Week: First week of June
- Annual Pony Penning: Last consecutive Wednesday and Thursday in July
- Beach Cleanup: One Saturday in mid- to late September
- National Wildlife Refuge Week: Second week of October
- Waterfowl Week Celebration: Thanksgiving week

AREA ACTIVITIES

- Bird-watching
- Biking
- Canoeing
- Hiking
- Photography
- Beachcombing
- Shell collecting
- Interpretive walks
- Surf fishing, clamming, crabbing
- Deer and waterfowl hunting
- Wildlife tours
- Swimming

WILDLIFE-VIEWING ETIQUETTE

- Be considerate of other visitors.
- Use designated parking areas.
- Don't feed or handle the ponies or other wildlife.
- Stay off the dunes. Use paths provided through sensitive habitats.
- Report unusual animal behavior potentially indicative of illness.
- Stay out of areas marked "Closed."
- Leave pets at home to avoid stressing wildlife. Pets are not allowed on the refuge.
- Remove trash and place in appropriate containers.
- Drive slowly and remain alert.
- Leave plants, animals, and historic artifacts undisturbed.

MAKING YOUR TRIP A SAFE ONE

- Protect yourself from the sun with sunscreen, a hat, sunglasses, and light-colored pants and a long-sleeved shirt.

- Keep a safe distance from wildlife.

- Be alert around traffic.

- Avoid poison ivy. Watch where you walk and put your hands.

- To avoid insect bites, use repellents. Wear light-colored clothing (long-sleeved shirts and long pants). Avoid perfumes.

- Minimize potential exposure to Lyme disease. This serious illness is transmitted by small deer ticks the size of a pinhead. Protect against bites as directed in the preceding bulleted item. Check for ticks after outings. If a tick is found, save it in case symptoms develop and the doctor wants to confirm your exposure to Lyme disease. If a bull's-eye-shaped rash or flu symptoms appear after a bite, seek medical attention immediately.

HOW CAN YOU HELP?

- Purchase a Golden Eagle Pass or Federal Duck Stamp.

- Visit wildlife refuges and parks regularly.

- Plant trees and employ land-use practices that prevent erosion.

- Minimize usage of pesticides and herbicides. Select natural alternatives.

- Landscape your home with native plant species beneficial to wildlife.

- Volunteer your services to a local wildlife refuge or park.

- Share your enthusiasm for wildlife with your friends, work associates, and family.

- Educate the young to respect and value wildlife.

- Support local legislation and organizations working to preserve critical wildlife habitat.

- Recycle renewable materials.

NEARBY WILDLIFE-VIEWING AREAS

- Assateague Island National Seashore, Md. and Va.
- Back Bay NWR, Va.
- Blackwater NWR, Md.
- Bombay Hook NWR, Del.
- Cape May NWR, N.J.
- Chesapeake Bay Environmental Center, Md.
- Eastern Neck NWR, Md.
- Eastern Shore of Virginia NWR, Va.
- Edwin B. Forsythe NWR, N.J.
- Fisherman Island NWR, Va.
- Great Dismal Swamp NWR, Va.
- Prime Hook NWR, Del.

Acknowledgments and Dedications

To the refuge staff members for their friendship and assistance.

To the Chincoteague Natural History Association for support of this book project.

To my parents for giving me an appreciation of nature and the courage to pursue my dreams.

To John Buckalew (pictured here), the first manager of Chincoteague National Wildlife Refuge, my mentor and friend.

ISBN-10: 1-56579-517-2 / ISBN-13: 978-1-56579-517-4

Text and photography copyright: Irene Hinke-Sacilotto, 2005. All rights reserved.

Editor: Jenna Samelson Browning

Design and Production: Craig Keyzer

Published by:
Westcliffe Publishers, Inc.
P.O. Box 1261
Englewood, CO 80150

Printed in China by Hing Yip Printing Company Limited

Library of Congress Cataloging-in-Publication Data:
Hinke-Sacilotto, Irene.
  Chincoteague National Wildlife Refuge : an ecological treasure / photography and text by Irene Hinke-Sacilotto.
     p. cm.
  ISBN 1-56579-517-2 (pbk.)
  1. Chincoteague National Wildlife Refuge (Va. and Md.) 2. Chincoteague National Wildlife Refuge (Va. and Md.)--Pictorial works. I. Title.
  QL84.22.V8H56 2005
  508.752'21--dc22   2004019369